Pennie Stoyles

The A–Z of
Health

Volume 2 C–E

Smart Apple Media
P.O. Box 3263
Mankato, MN, 56002

First published in 2010 by
MACMILLAN EDUCATION AUSTRALIA PTY LTD
15–19 Claremont St, South Yarra, Australia 3141

Visit our web site at www.macmillan.com.au or go directly to www.macmillanlibrary.com.au

Associated companies and representatives throughout the world.

Copyright © Pennie Stoyles 2010

Library of Congress Cataloging-in-Publication Data

Stoyles, Pennie.
    The A-Z of health / Pennie Stoyles.
        p. cm.
    Includes index.
    ISBN 978-1-59920-541-0 (library binding)
    ISBN 978-1-59920-542-7 (library binding)
    ISBN 978-1-59920-543-4 (library binding)
    ISBN 978-1-59920-544-1 (library binding)
    ISBN 978-1-59920-545-8 (library binding)
    ISBN 978-1-59920-546-5 (library binding)
    1. Medicine, Popular—Encyclopedias, Juvenile. 2. Health—Encyclopedias, Juvenile. I. Title.
    RC81.A2S76 2011
616.003--dc22

                                                                    2009038467

Edited by Julia Carlomagno and Gill Owens
Text and cover design by Ivan Finnegan, iF Design
Page layout by Raul Diche
Photo research by Legend Images
Illustrations by Andy Craig and Nives Porcellato, except for pp. 12, 30 (Guy Holt); p. 16 (Jeff Lang);
p. 22 (Alan Laver, Shelly Communications)

Manufactured in China by Macmillan Production (Asia) Ltd.
Kwun Tong, Kowloon, Hong Kong
Supplier Code: CP December 2009

Acknowledgments

The author and the publisher are grateful to the following for permission to reproduce copyright material:

Front cover photo of a teenager sneezing (or boy with a cold?) © 2008 Jupiterimages Corporation

Photographs courtesy of:
AAP Image/Jack Tran, 25; Brand X, 8; © Gideon Mendel/Corbis, 24; © Laura Dwight/Corbis, 19 (top); Gallo
Images/Getty Images, 20; © 2008 Jupiterimages Corporation, 10; Portrait of Professor Fred Hollows, Australian
of the Year in 1990, courtesy of National Library of Australia, 31 (bottom); National Library of Medicine,
Images from the History of Medicine (IHM), 9, 12 (left), 19 (bottom); Photolibrary/Aflo Foto Agency, 28;
Photolibrary/Banana Stock, 14; Photolibrary/Corbis, 23; Photolibrary/Russ Curtis, 13; Photolibrary/Heiner
Heine, 31 (top); Photolibrary/SPL, 27; Photolibrary/Brian Bell/SPL, 5; Photolibrary/CNRI/SPL, 6; Photolibrary/
Dr HC.Robinson/SPL, 7; Photolibrary/Science Source, 26; © Marc Dietrich/Shutterstock, 15 (bottom left);
© Elena Elisseeva/Shutterstock, 17; © greenland/Shutterstock, 11; © Lyckaro/Shutterstock, 15 (top); © Jozsef
Szasz-Fabian/Shutterstock, 21; © Dave Thompson/Shutterstock, 15 (bottom right).

Health

Welcome to the exciting world of health.

The A–Z of Health is about the healthy functioning of the body and mind. Health can mean:

- physical and mental health, including different body processes
- diseases and illnesses that affect health and well-being
- drugs, treatments, and ways to stay healthy

Volume 2 C–E   Health

They Said It!

"Early to bed and early to rise makes a man healthy, wealthy, and wise."

Benjamin Franklin, American philosopher and inventor

Cancer

Cancer is a disease in which the body's cells grow in an abnormal, uncontrollable way. There are hundreds of different types of cancer.

How Cancer Works

Cancer develops when the body's cells stop working properly and start to multiply more quickly than they should. In a healthy person, different types of cells perform different tasks. Nerve cells carry messages to and from the brain, skin cells protect the organs, and blood cells carry oxygen to organs. As these cells die, they are replaced by new cells. In a person with cancer, normal cells become cancerous, and they multiply quickly and live longer than normal cells. Over time, they may spread throughout the body until it cannot function properly.

Types of Cancer

Cancer can develop anywhere in the body. Some cancer cells grow in clumps called tumors. If cancer cells break away from a tumor, they can enter the bloodstream and travel to other parts of the body, where they may form new tumors. Cancer can also develop in the blood, which is constantly circulating around the body.

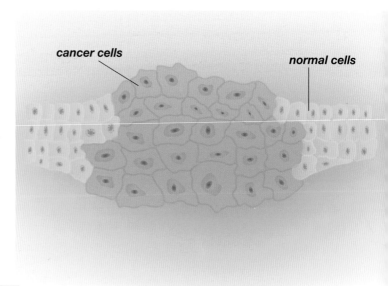

cancer cells

normal cells

A clump of cancer cells is called a tumor.

Did You Know?

Scientists are searching for new drugs to fight cancer. Many of these drugs use chemicals produced by sea creatures, bacteria, and plants.

Causes of Cancer

The causes of some cancers are known, while the causes of others are still undiscovered. A thing that causes cancer is called a **carcinogen** (say kah-SIN-uh-JUHN). Cigarette smoke is a carcinogen, as are some **viruses**.

Treating and Curing Cancer

It is difficult to treat and cure cancer. Doctors can sometimes perform surgery to remove a tumor. Some patients undergo chemotherapy, in which chemicals are used to kill cancer cells, or radiotherapy, in which **radiation** is used to kill cancer cells. However, these treatments can damage healthy cells as well.

Scientists are working to develop vaccines, which are treatments that will prevent cancers from developing.

HEALTH PROFESSIONALS: Oncologists

Oncologists (say ong-KOL-uh-GISTS) are doctors who specialize in treating people with cancer. They perform tests to determine whether a person has cancer and then decide which method will be most effective in treating it.

GLOSSARY WORDS

carcinogen	a substance that can cause cancer
viruses	microscopic living particles that stop cells from working properly
radiation	energy that travels in waves or particles

Chicken Pox

Chicken pox is a very **contagious** disease that mainly infects children.

The Varicella-zoster Virus

Chicken pox is caused by the varicella-zoster virus (VZV). When people with chicken pox sneeze, cough, or touch someone else, they can pass on this virus.

In the past, parents may have been relieved if their child caught VZV and developed chicken pox, as it meant the child would most likely not get chicken pox as an adult. Today, there is a **vaccine** for VZV, and children who receive it will never have chicken pox.

Symptoms of Chicken Pox

Symptoms of chicken pox usually develop about two weeks after a person is infected. First, an infected person will develop a fever and a sore throat. Then itchy red spots appear on the skin, which last for one or two weeks. Most people will only get chicken pox once in their lives, because the body develops **immunity** to it.

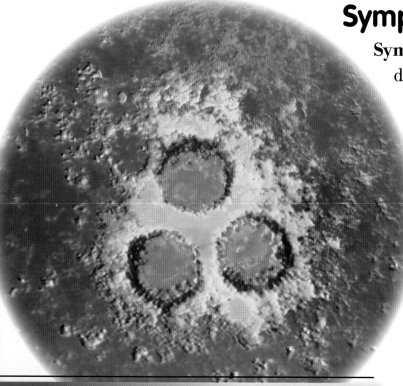

The VZV virus (shown in red in this enlargement) causes chicken pox and another disease, called herpes.

Did You Know?

Chicken pox is found in every country of the world.

Chicken Pox in Adults

Chicken pox can have much more serious effects in adults. It is particularly dangerous for women who are pregnant. If they get chicken pox early in their pregnancy, their babies can be born with abnormal arms, legs, eyesight, or hearing, and even with brain damage.

Adults who catch VZV a second time may develop a disease called shingles. Shingles is a painful skin rash that comes and goes. It is most common in people who are 50 years and older.

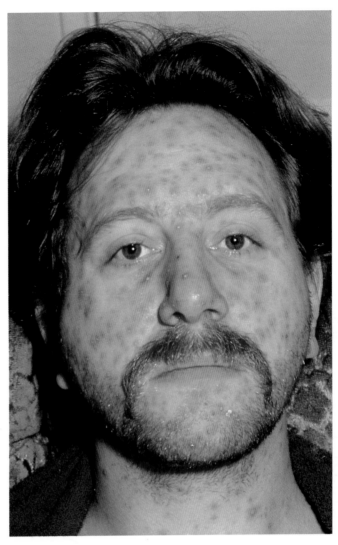

People with chicken pox develop itchy red spots on their skin.

Did You Know?

No one knows how chicken pox got its name. Some people think it is because the red spots look like the sufferer has been pecked by a chicken.

GLOSSARY WORDS

contagious	passes easily from one person to another
vaccine	a small dose of a virus or bacteria injected into patients to help their bodies fight off disease
symptoms	signs that a person may be suffering from a particular disease or illness
immunity	a natural protection from a disease

Cholesterol

Cholesterol (say kuh-LEST-uh-ROLL) is a type of fat. It is in the blood and the cells of the body. Cholesterol is also in some of the foods people eat.

Functions of Cholesterol

Cholesterol performs many important functions in the body. The body makes cholesterol in order to:

- keep nerves and **cell membranes** healthy
- make digestive juices that help break down food
- change into vitamin D, which keeps bones healthy

Types of Cholesterol

Doctors test for "good" and "bad" cholesterol in the blood. "Bad" cholesterol builds up on the insides of **blood vessels**. "Good" cholesterol helps to break down buildup of cholesterol in the blood vessels.

If eaten regularly, foods such as hamburgers and fries can increase the level of "bad" cholesterol in the blood.

Nikolai Anichkov (1885–1964)

Russian medical scientist Nikolai Anichkov discovered the link between cholesterol and the narrowing and hardening of blood vessels.

Plaque

A buildup of cholesterol is called plaque. Plaque can cause blood vessels to narrow, which means that the heart must beat harder to pump blood around the body. This can lead to high blood pressure and an increased risk of **heart attack**. Plaque can also break off and travel in the bloodstream, blocking smaller blood vessels elsewhere in the body. This can lead to a heart attack or a **stroke**.

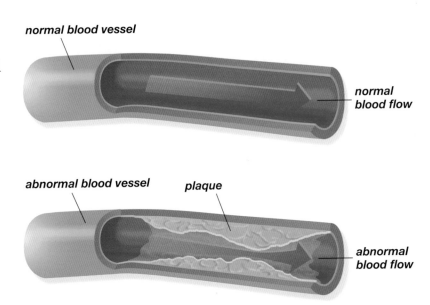

normal blood vessel

normal blood flow

abnormal blood vessel *plaque*

abnormal blood flow

Blood can travel easily through a healthy blood vessel (top), but has difficulty traveling through a blood vessel blocked by cholesterol plaque (bottom).

Keeping Cholesterol Levels Healthy

People can change their eating and drinking habits to keep their cholesterol levels healthy. People with high cholesterol levels should exercise regularly and only occasionally eat high-cholesterol foods, such as butter, cheese, eggs, and deep-fried food. People should also avoid factors that are known to increase cholesterol, such as smoking, feeling stressed over a long period of time, and drinking large amounts of alcohol.

Did You Know?

Some margarines, yogurts, and breakfast cereals have a substance called phytosterol (say fuy-TO-stuh-ROLL) added to them. Phytosterol helps to lower cholesterol in the blood.

GLOSSARY WORDS

cell membranes	thin layers of tissue surrounding cells
blood vessels	tubes, such as veins or arteries, which blood travels through
heart attack	damage to the heart that occurs when blood flow to the heart is reduced or blocked
stroke	brain damage that occurs when blood flow to the brain is reduced or blocked

Colds

Colds are infections in the nose and throat. There are more than 200 **viruses** that cause colds.

Catching a Cold

When a person has a cold, his or her nose contains thousands of cold viruses. Whenever the person sneezes or blows the nose, these viruses spread through the air and can be inhaled by anyone nearby. People are most contagious for the first two or three days after they have caught a cold. However, **symptoms** do not begin to show until after this time. This means that many people can pass cold viruses on to others before they even realize they are sick.

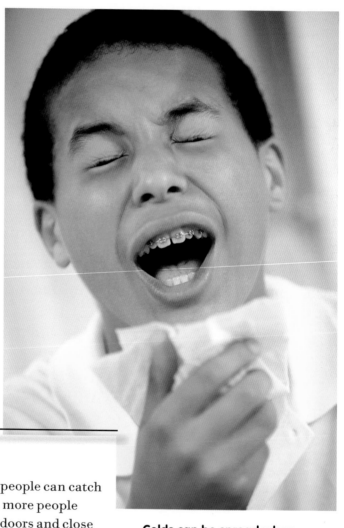

Symptoms of a Cold

Symptoms of a cold include itchy and runny noses, sore throats, and coughing. Itchy noses and throats are often the first symptoms of a cold. Soon after, a person's nose may begin to run and he or she may start to sneeze. The person's nose may block up completely and the person may develop a cough.

Did You Know?

Colds are not related to the cold weather, as people can catch them in both summer and winter. However, more people get colds in winter because they are often indoors and close to other people. This means that cold-causing viruses have more opportunity to spread among people.

Colds can be spread when someone with cold viruses in his or her nose sneezes.

Treating Colds

Doctors can **prescribe** drugs to treat the symptoms of a cold, but these do not shorten the length of a cold. **Antibiotics** (say an-TIE-buy-OT-iks) cannot be used to treat colds because antibiotics only kill bacteria, not viruses. The best treatment for colds is often to get plenty of rest and to drink lots of liquids while the body fights the virus.

A Cure for Colds?

There is currently no cure for colds. While scientists have been able to develop vaccines against some viruses, there are too many types of cold viruses to vaccinate people against every one. Scientists would have to develop more than 200 vaccines, and people would have to have all of them in order to avoid getting a cold. This would be expensive for patients and time-consuming for doctors.

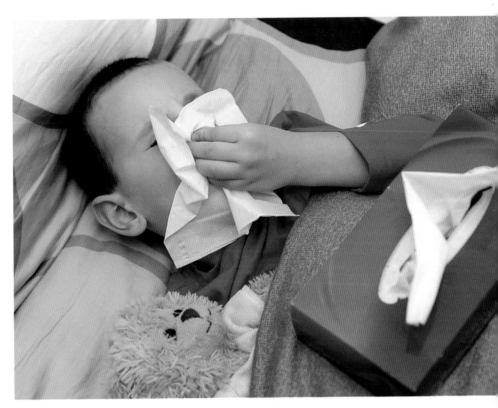

People usually recover from a cold in seven to ten days if they make sure that they get enough rest.

Did You Know?

Cold sores are itchy sores that can develop around the mouth. They are caused by a different virus from those that cause colds.

GLOSSARY WORDS

viruses	microscopic living particles that stop cells from working properly
symptoms	signs that a person may be suffering from a particular disease or illness
prescribe	recommend a drug to be taken to treat a particular illness
antibiotics	substances that can kill microscopic cells called bacteria

Diabetes

Diabetes (say duy-UH-beet-EEZ) is a disease in which a person has too much sugar in his or her blood.

Glucose and Insulin

When food is digested, a sugar called glucose gets into the blood. Glucose is carried to cells in the body, providing them with energy to work and grow. A **hormone** called insulin, which is made in the pancreas, helps move glucose from the blood into the cells. People with diabetes do not produce enough insulin, or their cells do not allow the insulin to do its job properly, or both.

Types of Diabetes

There are two main types of diabetes.

- Type 1 diabetes is sometimes called **juvenile** diabetes because it develops in children. Their bodies stop making insulin, and they have to have insulin injections once or twice a day for the rest of their lives.

- Type 2 diabetes is sometimes called adult diabetes because it usually affects adults. Their bodies make less insulin, and their cells do not respond normally to insulin. People can often control adult diabetes by eating particular foods and leading healthy lifestyles.

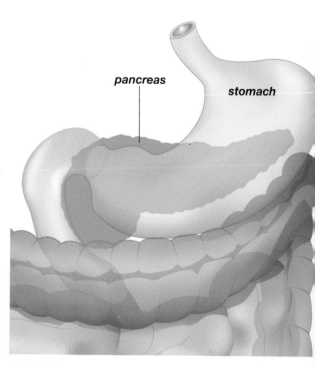

pancreas

stomach

Insulin is made in the pancreas, a gland that sits behind the stomach.

Frederick Sanger (1918–)

British scientist Frederick Sanger is the only person to win two Nobel Prizes in Chemistry. He won in 1958 for discovering the chemical structure of insulin. He won again in 1980 for discovering how to read information held in genes.

Hyperglycemia and Hypoglycemia

People with diabetes may experience hyperglycemia (say hy-PER-gluy-SEEM-ee-AH) or hypoglycemia (say hy-PO-gluy-SEEM-ee-AH). Hyperglycemia is caused by having too much sugar in the blood. **Symptoms** include being thirsty and tired, wanting to go to the toilet often, and losing weight. Many **diabetics** may experience these symptoms before being diagnosed with diabetes.

Diabetics who take insulin sometimes don't have enough sugar in their blood. This is called hypoglycemia. Symptoms include trembling, sweating, hunger, drowsiness, and confusion.

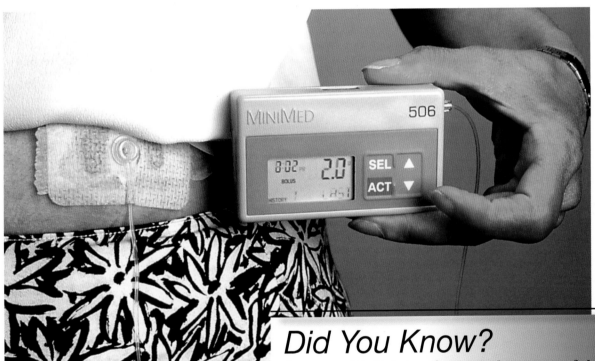

Some people with diabetes wear insulin pumps, which are devices that pump insulin through a small tube and into the body.

Did You Know?

A person with diabetes often tests the amount of glucose in the blood by using blood glucose meters. The person pricks his or her finger and places a drop of blood onto a card, which is read by the meter. The reading allows the person to see if he or she needs to adjust his or her diet or take insulin.

GLOSSARY WORDS

hormone	a chemical that controls how the body works
juvenile	to do with children
symptoms	signs that a person may be suffering from a particular disease or illness
diabetics	people with diabetes

13

Diet

Diet is the food and drink that people eat to grow and to fuel the body.

A Balanced Diet

A balanced diet keeps the body healthy. It contains the right amounts of different **nutrients** needed to provide energy and to help the body to grow.

- Sugar and starch provide energy. Fruit, vegetables, and cereals are high in sugar and starch. They also contain cellulose, which helps the **digestive system** work.

- Proteins build muscles and keep body processes functioning. Meat, fish, eggs, and dairy foods are high in proteins.

- Fats provide energy and help cells to work properly. Butter, oil, and margarine are high in fats.

- Vitamins and minerals each perform a different function in the body, such as helping organs and cells function. Many foods contain certain vitamins and minerals.

Dieticians advise people on what foods are right for their bodies.

HEALTH PROFESSIONALS: Dieticians

Dieticians are trained to know the nutrients in food and the functions they perform. Dieticians know how to determine the best diet for people in different situations, including athletes, sick people, and overweight people.

Energy in Food

The energy in food is measured in calories (Cal). Foods with high levels of fat and sugar, such as potato chips and candy, contain large amounts of energy. When these foods are digested, the body uses the energy to move and grow. However, if a person consumes large amounts these foods, there will be too much energy for the body to use and the excess energy will be converted into fat.

Daily Food Intake

Doctors and dieticians work together to suggest the proper amounts of different foods that people should eat every day, depending on their ages and body weights.

An apple and a glass of low-fat milk contain about 95 calories of energy, while a bag of potato chips and a soda contain about 380 calories of energy, which is almost a quarter of the energy the body needs each day.

Did You Know?

Some people try unusual diets for a short time to lose weight quickly. These diets might involve only eating one food, or one food group. They are hard to maintain and people often put on more weight when they return to eating normally.

GLOSSARY WORDS

nutrients	food or chemicals that the body needs to survive
digestive system	a system of organs and glands that processes food and turns it into energy

Digestion

Digestion is the process by which the body extracts the nutrients and energy from food and eliminates waste.

How Digestion Works

Digestion begins in the mouth, where food is broken up through chewing. Saliva, or spit, is a digestive juice that begins the chemical breakdown of food. Food is then mixed with more digestive juices in the stomach. Nutrients are absorbed into the blood in the small intestine and carried to the liver. The liver also produces digestive juices that it squirts into the small intestine. By the time food reaches the large intestine, it is mainly waste. The body absorbs water from the waste before passing it out as **feces**.

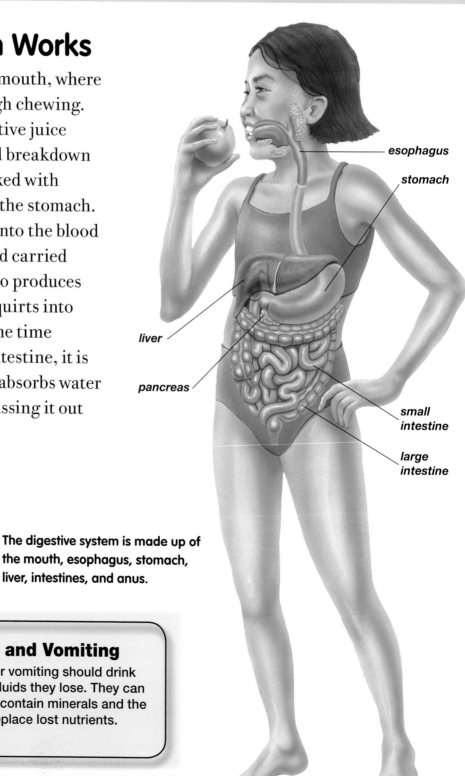

esophagus

stomach

liver

pancreas

small intestine

large intestine

The digestive system is made up of the mouth, esophagus, stomach, liver, intestines, and anus.

FIRST AID

Treating Diarrhea and Vomiting

People with bad **diarrhea** or vomiting should drink lots of water to replace the fluids they lose. They can also have special drinks that contain minerals and the sugar glucose, to give them energy and replace lost nutrients.

Gastroenteritis

Gastroenteritis (say gas-TROH-en-TUH-ruy-TUS) is an **inflammation** of the digestive system. It can be caused by bacteria, **viruses**, or other microscopic parasites. The **symptoms** of gastro include bad stomach pains, diarrhea, nausea, and vomiting. It is transmitted through touch and sharing food.

Constipation

Constipation is a condition in which people have difficulty passing feces. It is caused by a lack of fiber in the diet or by taking certain medications.

Washing hands after using the toilet helps prevent the spread of germs that cause gastro.

HEALTH PROFESSIONALS: Gastroenterologists

Gastroenterologists (say gas-TROH-ent-UH-roll-OH-gists) are doctors who specialize in conditions and diseases of the digestive system. They sometimes use special tubes with tiny cameras, called colonoscopes and gastroscopes, to examine a person's digestive system.

GLOSSARY WORDS

feces	waste material that comes from the intestines
inflammation	redness, swelling, and pain caused by an injury to the body
viruses	microscopic living particles that stop cells from working properly
symptoms	signs that a person may be suffering from a particular disease or illness
diarrhea	a disorder in the intestines that causes runny feces

Down Syndrome

Down syndrome is a **genetic disorder** that occurs when a person is born with an extra chromosome (say kroh-MUH-sohm). It is the most common genetic disorder.

Chromosomes

Chromosomes are found in every cell in the body, and they carry information about all of a person's physical characteristics. Most people have 23 pairs of chromosomes, and the pairs are numbered from 1 to 23. One chromosome in each pair is inherited from the mother and one from the father.

Chromosomes in Down Syndrome

People with Down syndrome have three chromosomes instead of two at chromosome pair 21. Doctors believe that the extra chromosome is carried either in the mother's egg or the father's sperm, but they do not know why.

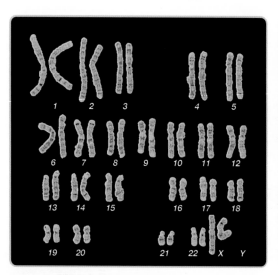
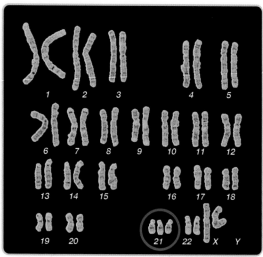

While most people have 23 pairs of chromosomes (left), people with Down syndrome have a third chromosome in pair 21 (right).

Did You Know?

Women who have babies when they are more than 40 years old have an increased chance of having a baby with Down syndrome.

Symptoms of Down Syndrome

The **symptoms** of Down syndrome can be both physical and intellectual. People with Down syndrome often have small mouths and hands, as well as upward-slanting eyes. Their arms and legs may also be shorter than others'. Some suffer from heart problems, which mean that they may not live to old age. Many people with Down syndrome also have an intellectual disability, which means that it may take them longer to learn how to do certain tasks.

Families may have some children with Down syndrome and others without.

John Langdon Down (1828–1896)

John Langdon Down was a British doctor who worked to improve treatments for children with intellectual disabilities. He published a description of Down syndrome in 1866, and the disorder is named in his honor.

GLOSSARY WORDS

genetic disorder	a disorder that is caused by a problem in the genes, which make up the chromosomes
symptoms	signs that a person may be suffering from a particular disease or illness

Drugs

Drugs are substances that people take to prevent or to cure a disease or to change the way they feel.

Types of Drugs

There are many types of drugs, and the word is used to mean different things. Drugs can be medicines that a doctor prescribes to treat common illnesses. Drugs can be illegal substances, such as **heroin** and **marijuana** (say mar-UH-war-NAH). Drugs can also be legal substances, such as alcohol, coffee, and cigarettes.

Illegal drugs

Many illegal drugs, such as heroin and marijuana, may make people feel good for a short time, but they are very addictive and dangerous to their health. Governments pass laws to make it illegal for people to use these drugs.

Police seize illegal drugs so that people in the community cannot take them and develop addictions.

Did You Know?

When Coca-Cola™ was first released, it contained a drug called cocaine, which is now illegal in most countries. This is where the "Coca" part of the name comes from. Cocaine was removed from the drink in 1903.

Legal Drugs

Alcohol, cigarettes, and coffee are legal drugs that change the way the body works. Alcohol contains a substance called ethanol, and when people drink large amounts of alcohol the ethanol affects their brains. Often, people who are drunk cannot move, think, or speak properly. Cigarettes contain the stimulant nicotine and coffee contains the stimulant caffeine. Stimulants speed up physical and mental processes in the body for a short period of time.

Some legal substances, such as coffee, alcohol, and cigarettes, can affect the way the body works.

Addiction and Overdose

Many drugs are addictive, which means that a person who is in the habit of taking them may find it very difficult to stop. Sometimes people are tempted to take too much of a dangerous drug, which can lead to an **overdose**. People who overdose can get very sick and may die if they do not receive medical treatment quickly.

Did You Know?

People who have had surgery are often given painkillers by their doctors. The dose is gradually reduced as the patient gets better so that they do not become addicted.

GLOSSARY WORDS

heroin   a drug made from morphine
marijuana   a drug made from the leaves of the cannabis plant
overdose   poisoning by taking a dangerous amount of a drug

Ee | Ears

Ears are sense organs that allow people to hear. They also help people keep their balance.

How Ears Work

Ears collect sound waves, transfer them to the head, and then turn them into nerve signals that the brain can read.

Parts of an Ear

An ear has three parts.

- The outer ear can be seen on the outside of the head.

- The middle ear contains the **eardrum** and three tiny bones that transfer sound vibrations to the head.

- The inner ear, or cochlea (say KOK-lee-uh), turns sound vibrations into nerve signals. It is full of liquid, which helps with balance.

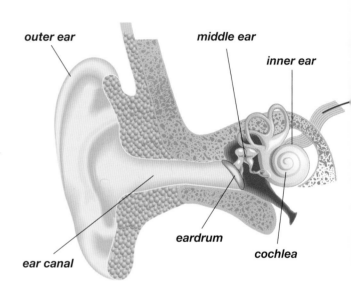

outer ear   middle ear

inner ear

eardrum

ear canal

cochlea

The human ear has three parts: the outer ear, the middle ear, and the inner ear.

Earwax

Ears make earwax, a substance that keeps ears healthy. Earwax contains special chemicals that fight infections. It also collects dirt to help keep **ear canals** clean. People should not clean their ears with cotton-tipped sticks as this pushes the earwax against the eardrums and blocks the ear canals.

Did You Know?

The smallest bone in the body is the stapes, or stirrup bone, which is one of the three bones in the middle ear.

Ear Health Problems

Two common health problems associated with ears are hearing loss and ear infections. Hearing loss can be caused by listening to loud music or hearing loud noises. People should make sure that the volume is not too high when listening to music through earphones, and use ear protectors when they know they will be exposed to loud noises.

Ear infections are caused when infectious bacteria move from the nose to the ear. The middle ear is connected to the back of the nose by a tube called the Eustachian (say yooh-STAY-shee-un) tube. If a person has a cold and a blocked nose, the infection may move up this tube and enter the middle ear. People who have fluid in their middle ear sometimes have ear tubes inserted into the middle ear to help drain the fluid.

Listening to loud music or any loud noises can cause hearing loss.

HEALTH PROFESSIONALS: Audiologists

Audiologists assess hearing problems, work out what sorts of hearing aids people might need, fit hearing aids, and teach patients how to use them properly. They also provide advice on how to prevent hearing loss.

GLOSSARY WORDS

eardrum   thin, tightly stretched tissue in the middle ear
ear canals   passages between the outer ear and the eardrum

Epidemic

An epidemic (say epi-DEM-ik) is an **outbreak** of a disease in which many people become affected during a short period of time.

The Spread of Disease

Epidemics occur when a disease spreads quickly through a community. Disease can spread because there are a lot of people living close together, there are poor **hygiene** and health controls, or the disease is a new **strain** that humans have not developed immunity to. Many epidemics occur after natural disasters, such as earthquakes and hurricanes, which often damage electricity, water, and sewer systems. If these systems break down, disease can spread quickly, and there may not be enough hospitals or drugs to treat patients.

Preventing Epidemics

Epidemics can be prevented with proper hygiene and health controls. People with some types of contagious diseases should stay at home or in the hospital so that they do not infect others. People can also be vaccinated against some contagious diseases. This prevents them from catching the disease and passing it on to others.

These people are marching in support of people with HIV/AIDS, a damaging disease that has become a global epidemic.

Did You Know?

Around 1400, an epidemic called the Black Death traveled through Europe and Asia. It is believed to have killed between one-quarter and one-half of all the people in Europe.

The Spanish Flu

Between 1918 and 1920, there was a major epidemic known as the Spanish flu. It was caused by a severe strain of the influenza, or flu, **virus**. It spread to many countries around the world, and is estimated to have killed between 20 million and 100 million people. Some people believe that it was spread by soldiers who fought in Europe during World War I. When the soldiers returned home at the end of the war, they brought the disease with them.

The Spanish flu is sometimes called "the flu pandemic." A pandemic is an epidemic that spreads to many different countries in a short space of time.

In 2009, some people wore face masks to prevent the spread of the swine flu virus.

HEALTH PROFESSIONALS: Epidemiologists

Epidemiologists study contagious diseases and epidemics to determine how disease affects large groups of people. They also examine how factors such as diet and smoking affect populations.

GLOSSARY WORDS

outbreak	a sudden and unexpected occurrence
hygiene	practices for keeping the body healthy
strain	type of a particular disease
virus	microscopic living particles that stop cells from working properly

Epilepsy

Epilepsy (say epi-LEP-see) is a **brain disorder** that causes fits, known as seizures. People suffering from epilepsy are known as epileptics.

Epilepsy and the Brain

The brain is made up of millions of nerve cells that control the body's actions, thoughts, and emotions. Messages travel through the nerve cells via chemical and electrical signals. If these signals in the brain are suddenly disrupted, it can cause a seizure.

Seizures

A seizure is a sudden disruption in the brain that often causes physical responses, such as **convulsions**. During a seizure, an epileptic may have unusual and uncontrollable movements, and strange feelings.

Different sorts of epileptic seizures cause different physical responses. Large seizures may cause epileptics to become very stiff, fall over, and then experience jerky body movements. Other seizures may cause epileptics to become limp and fall down. Small seizures may cause epileptics to stare into the distance for a short time with flickering eyelids. Following a seizure, epileptics often feel confused or disoriented.

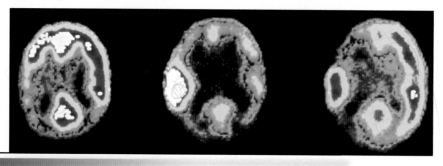

Brain scans are used to study the brains of people with epilepsy. The image on the left shows no seizures, but the white area in the middle image and the red areas in the right image show severe seizure activity.

Did You Know?

Many famous people have suffered from epilepsy, including Roman emperor Julius Caesar, artist Leonardo da Vinci, and scientist Thomas Edison.

Causes of Epilepsy

Epilepsy can be caused by a range of factors. Some people may be born with a brain abnormality that causes epilepsy. Sometimes epilepsy can develop as a result of a brain injury or infection, or through the use of certain drugs, such as alcohol. In many cases, doctors are unsure why patients have developed epilepsy.

Treating Epilepsy

While there is no cure for epilepsy, there are drugs that can help control seizures or stop them completely. Many children who suffer from epilepsy also find that their seizures occur less often as they get older. Adult epileptics who are at risk of having seizures often do not drive cars or operate heavy machinery, as it would put them in danger if they had a seizure while doing so.

FIRST AID +

Helping with Seizures

If a person has a seizure, call for help and then protect the person by moving objects out of his or her way. If the person has fallen down, put something soft under his head. Try to roll the person on his or her side so that there is less likelihood of choking. It is useful to time how long the seizure lasts, as the longer the seizure, the more dangerous it may be for the person's brain.

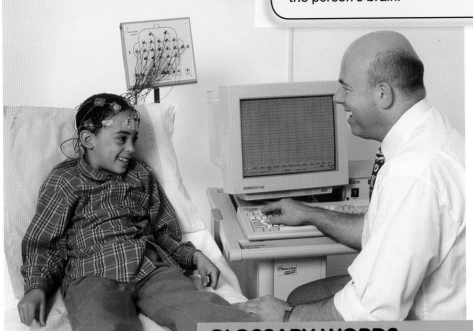

People with epilepsy may have their brain activity monitored in the hospital by doctors.

GLOSSARY WORDS

brain disorder	a disorder that occurs when the brain has difficulty processing certain types of information normally
convulsions	sudden, uncontrollable body movements

Exercise

Exercise is any activity that uses energy, increases fitness, and strengthens the muscles and bones.

Using Energy

People need energy to exercise, and the more exercise they do, the more energy they need. Energy comes from food. If a person eats some food and then exercises, he or she will use up some or all of the energy in that food. If a person eats some food and does not exercise, the body may convert some or all of that energy to fat.

Increasing Physical Fitness

People usually exercise to increase fitness. People who are fit have healthy hearts, blood, and lungs. They are not **overweight**, and they have reasonably strong muscles.

When a person is fit, his or her body is more able to fight off disease and recover quickly from injuries. Physically fit people can play sports without getting tired easily.

When people exercise regularly, their brains produces chemicals called endorphins, which make them feel happy.

Did You Know?

One way to measure fitness is to see how quickly someone recovers after exercise. Fit people should feel their heart rate return to normal a few minutes after they stop exercising.

Strengthening Muscles

Exercise makes the muscles stronger, and some people do specific exercises to strengthen particular muscles. One of the most important muscles in the body is the heart. People strengthen their hearts by doing at least 20 minutes of exercise that increases their heart rate.

Strengthening Bones

Some forms of exercise help strengthen bones. Weight-bearing exercises, such as running, jumping, climbing stairs, and dancing, involve lifting the whole weight of the body. Every time the feet hit the ground, the bones are stressed a little and the body works to make them stronger.

muscle pulls against the bone and becomes stronger

People who run regularly put stress on their bones and muscles. Over time, their bodies work to make these bones and muscles stronger.

HEALTH PROFESSIONALS: Exercise Physiologists

Exercise physiologists are trained to design exercise programs to meet different people's needs. They develop exercises for professional athletes, people recovering from injuries, and people who want to lose weight or improve their fitness.

GLOSSARY WORD

overweight   having too much body fat

Eyes

Eyes are the sense organs that allow people to see.

How Eyes Work

Eyes take in detailed three-dimensional colored information and transfer it to the brain. The cornea and lens at the front of the eye focus an image on the retina at the back of the eye. The retina contains more than 30 million light-sensitive cells that change the image into nerve impulses, which travel to the brain along the optic nerve.

Looking After Eyes

To look after their eyes, people should:

- never look directly at the sun as sunlight can damage the retina
- wear sunglasses on sunny days, to block the sun's harmful **ultraviolet rays**
- always read in well-lit places
- rest the eyes regularly if reading or using a computer for long periods of time
- treat eye infections, such as **conjunctivitis**, immediately to prevent permanent eye damage

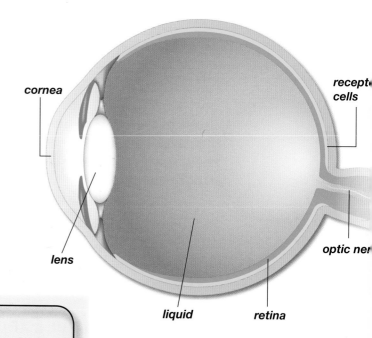

Light is focused on the retina, which sends information through the optic nerve to the brain.

cornea · lens · liquid · retina · recept cells · optic ner

FIRST AID

Protecting Eyes

People who work with dangerous liquids should always wear safety goggles. If people get dangerous liquids such as acid in their eyes, they should immediately wash their eyes under running water for up to 20 minutes.

Glaucoma

Glaucoma (say glaow-KOH-muh) is an eye disease that damages the optic nerve and can lead to blindness. People with glaucoma have too much liquid inside their eyeballs. This liquid causes the eyeball to change shape so that the retina does not function properly. People with glaucoma can have a very small field of vision.

Cataracts

Cataracts are an eye disease that can develop on the lens of the eye as people get older. The lens of the eye becomes milky and opaque, so that everything a person sees is blurred. Cataracts can be treated with a simple operation in which the milky lens is removed and replaced with a plastic lens.

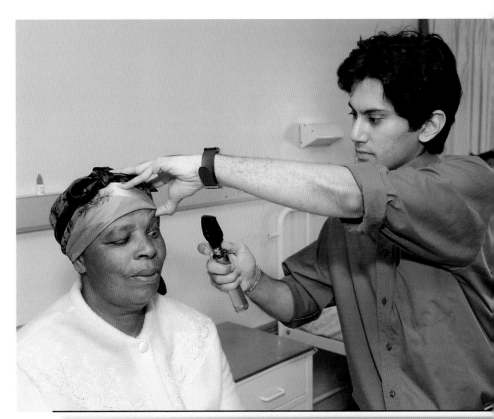

This doctor is examining a patient with cataracts.

Fred Hollows (1929–1993)

Ophthalmologist Fred Hollows was born in New Zealand but became an Australian citizen. He worked in Eritrea, Nepal, and Vietnam to train local doctors to operate on people with eye diseases. Today, The Fred Hollows Foundation carries on his work.

GLOSSARY WORDS

ultraviolet rays   invisible rays of light
conjunctivitis   an eye infection that causes eyes to become itchy, red, and swollen

Index

Page references in bold indicate that there is a full entry for that topic.